Acta, Non Verba

CW00550441

Beth Salmon

BookLeaf
Publishing

Acta, Non Verba © 2022 Beth Salmon

All rights reserved.

Beth Salmon asserts the moral right to be identified as author of this work.

Presentation by *BookLeaf Publishing*

Web: www.bookleafpub.com

E-mail: info@bookleafpub.com

ISBN: 978-93-95890-48-9

First edition 2022

DEDICATION

Dedicated to the memory of Brian Salmon. We love and miss you so much.

"You can only hope you've done more good than bad in this life".

ACKNOWLEDGEMENT

To my lovely parents, Bill & Cheryl - thank you for everything you have done for me.

To my Nan & Pops - thank you for always supporting me.

To my sisters - thank you for always putting up with me!

Thank you to my dear friends: Sam, Quiz Team and The Magnificent 6 (you know who you are) for simply being you.

Of course, to my favourite lizard. This one's for you.

G & A

Be my ocean and carry me away;
I long to be swept adrift by you.
I have never tasted love
But I imagine it like this;
A torment of sensations without words.
Your mind is my dearest friend,
Your touch, my favourite conversation.
I see the moon in your eyes,
How they glimmer when the light hits,
How they shine when you smile.
You make my heart skip a beat.
Every second spent with you is a gift.
I have found myself in you;
I did not believe in love at first sight
Until my eyes locked into yours.
I fell for your soul before I touched your skin.
I have lost a piece of my heart,
And it has found its way to you.

Stars

A thousand eyes
Glare at me from above,
They shimmer in the sky,
and watch my watch my every move.
Stars shine and light the empty void,
They acknowledge my mistakes
and help me grow.
I see you in them;
How they fill me with hope.
Light up the dark days,
Give me the strength to move forward.

Angel on the Avenue

On days like these, I find it hard
To believe you were ever even here,
But I don't think I could ever forget
Your lips, as soft and sweet as music.
You were my angel on the avenue,
I wish I could taste your lips again;
You could kill me with them.
I'm fed up of biting my own.
Calm my restless heart
With the unruly sea of you.
You are the perfect light,
As I wade through this sea of darkness.
I am buried under the need
To return to what was never meant to be.
Keep the key, but lock me in your box
and open it when you're lonely.
Like the next breath of smoke
From this cigarette,
You're killing me.

Unpredictable Storms

My body is a ship
That has finally anchored
Into the safe waters of your arms.

I feel safe here.

Yet still, I sometimes long
For open sea; mystery,
And unpredictable storms.

Autumn Leaf

Sadness grows within me
Like a tree grown from seed.

At first, slow and gentle
Then suddenly, stronger
More rapid growth.

An abundance of silence fills my lungs
and it threatens to wrap
it's bony fingers around my neck
and suffocate me.

The loneliness lives inside me
Meandering further out
Like the skeletal veins
of an autumn leaf.

Window to the Soul

If eyes are the window to the soul,
I could devour yours.
Eat your thoughts and consume you.
Hold me and you will feel how broken I am,
Fix me up
And make me one again.

Dandelion Clock

I have found myself very familiar with your
face,
The twisting tendrils of your hair.
I have been learning how to trust,
You have made my life
Feel new and free again.
My body entwined with yours,
I see a bloom of what is to come.
What is this feeling that grows inside me?
The fantasy of a gentle caress erupts within me,
This thing, this feeling;
Like a thousand tiny fairies
Dancing aimlessly
Around a dandelion clock.
At last
I feel
Peace.

Nineteen

Enclosed within these thin walls,
Increasingly familiar with the realms of my
mind.
I am learning how to
Climb my walls
Learning more about
Who I am each day.
How strange, to be living
Breathing
Aligned
With a dying world.

Darling Buds of Summer

Darling buds of summer
Call a song sweetly sung,
If it were not for you, my love,
Then I would sing for no-one.
For Mother Nature's song is heard
In the slowly swaying grass.
I'll bide my time like mulling wine
Until this comes to pass.
When it does, my dear, you'll know
Just what you mean to me.
With God's pure grace, I'll see your face,
Smiling gently back at me.
For time will pass; time will heal
And you'll know how you're adored.

Dark Days

Translucent skin, blue veins
Soon I will be cold again.
Crying on the bedroom floor,
Sick and tired of these games once more.
I can't take this again; life is rough,
But I'm sick to death of being tough.
Let me go, let me roam,
Let me navigate this world alone.
I am lonely, I am broken,
I fear my last words have been spoken.
Let me fall, deep, deep,
Further down to the deepest sleep.

Missing you comes in waves,
And tonight, I am drowning.

Cloud 9

I was visiting could nine.
Suddenly,
Brought back down to Earth.
Taken in by the belligerent sun
And swallowed whole.
The grey days become more frequent,
I shall never again
Undress the soft bud of a rose.
Instead, find me horizontally aligned,
A hurricane of thought
Hugging the corners of my messy bed.
The pages of my book lie sleeping
I flick them until my fingertips bleed
And serenity washes over me.

Poet's Urge

How can one resist
The poet's urge to love with language
To long for you with verse.
I beg you, this is not the end
Merely the first act.
The moon is an insomniac; so am I,
And I spend the night talking to her
About you.
I dare not close my eyes,
I cannot bear again
To slip, drown in an ocean of dreams.
Dreams of lost love, unrequited love,
Dreams of you.
I cannot help but slip in the darkness,
Splashing, crashing, screaming your name.
My eyes awaken to the light of day,
The moon smiles as she fades away.
Yet I cannot fade away the ashes of my burnt,
bruised heart.

Sorrow

One lonely magpie
Hops softly along the green blanket
yet still
the grass is hesitant to grow.

I am drowning in a lagoon
of desperation.

Lying on the hard floor
I gaze up at the grey sky,
Visions of bad days, sleepless night.

Unexpectedly, I am free.
A hit becomes a hand,
a hand; now, an arm.
My cuts and bruises become kisses.

Entwined together on the floor
I shut my eyes; darkness surrounds me,
and I feel a sense of comfort.

Another bird swoops in
and my sorrow turns to joy.

Hands

When we're apart
I hold your hand in my heart;
Finding you made up for everything
I lost along the way.
Things would get colder than ever
Without your hands to keep me warm.

Black Hole

There's an ocean inside of you,
All that I have is the desire
And willingness to explore
The very depths of you.
I am a black hole; you are the ocean.
It is dark here, and depth has no meaning.

I've seen rivers make valleys from mountains
And he is an ocean.
All I wanted was a drop of rain
But you gave me a hurricane.

I have loved you like the sea
So, if your soul should wander,
Let it wander back to me.

Sweet Delights

You are sweet delights
I have never tasted,
Colours I have never seen.
Your touch, electric on my skin
Was conjured up by the moon and stars.

Poetry

Our love is poetry
Flowing freely on the page.
I have never managed
to fit in anywhere,
Apart from your arms.

I am the horizon
and you are my sea.
Your depths match my own,
and, within them,
I feel I am home.

Daffodils

In a field full of daffodils
Pure and gold
I can only see you; your eyes
Brown as chestnuts.
Mother Nature surrounds me
But the only beauty I see
Is that of your soul.
My eyes are tainted
With sea blue waves
And grey rainy days,
Filled with a feeling
That's only for you.

Dreamers

Meet me under the moonlit sky;
If we cannot be as one,
Then let our eyes share the shimmering lights.
You are the calm in my chaos,
The sun in my storm.
You drew me in with an insatiable gravity;
I had no power against the pull of your desire.
Together, we are music.
Press play and let time give in
So we can waltz to the rhythm of us.
Darkness disappears when I touch you,
You have lightened up my life.
Distance between the stars
Makes constellations beautiful,
And when we come together again,
I will kiss you until the skies collapse.

For You

Fire lived within our first kiss
and I long to burnt by your touch again.
Kind kisses leave lips like rippling echoes,
You are a cascading stream
of all encompassing beauty
and I have lost myself in your flow.
Let me place my hand upon your chest,
Watch it rise and fall
in rhythm with the ocean.
I had never connected with another
who spoke my language; then
I met you.
Like a wave hitting the shore,
This feeling, it is gentle but fierce.
You are fluent in me, yet
It is your uniqueness, not our sameness
that makes you truly exceptional.

Cup of Love

I should have told you
that love is open,
around everywhere.
You always believed
that love is secret, hidden.
It isn't. And so,
I will let you drink
from the cup of my love.
As long as your heart is thirsty,
I will quench you.

Ingram Content Group UK Ltd.
Milton Keynes UK
UKHW020806020623
422771UK00015B/472